Property of

_____

Ellie Doodle

HOME NETWORKING INFORMATION

Internet Service Provider

`Account #

Phone# for Customer Service

Wireless Network Name (SSID)

Channel

Security Mode

WPA Shared Key

WEP Pass Phrase

**Modem Name &
Model #**

Serial #

IP Address

Mac Address

WAN IP Address

UserName

Password

WAN Settings

MAC Address

IP Address

Host Name

Domain Name

Subnet Mask

DNS Primary

DNS Secondary

Default Gateway

SOFTWARE INFORMATION

Software

License #

Purchase Date

Software

License #

Purchase Date

Software

License #

Purchase Date

Software

License #

Purchase Date

PASSWORDS

Software

License #

Purchase Date

Software

License #

Purchase Date

Software

License #

Purchase Date

Software

License #

Purchase Date

Website

Username

Password

Notes

Website

Username

Password

Notes

Website

Username

Password

Notes

Website

Username

Password

Notes

Website

Username

Password

Notes

Website

Username

Password

Notes

Website

Username

Password

Notes

Website

Username

Password

Notes

Website

Username

Password

Notes

Website

Username

Password

Notes

Website

Username

Password

Notes

Website

Username

Password

Notes

Website

Username

Password

Notes

Website

Username

Password

Notes

Website

Username

Password

Notes

Website

Username

Password

Notes

Website

Username

Password

Notes

Website

Username

Password

Notes

Website

Username

Password

Notes

Website

Username

Password

Notes

Website

Username

Password

Notes

Website

Username

Password

Notes

Website

Username

Password

Notes

Website

Username

Password

Notes

CD

Website

Username

Password

Notes

Website

Username

Password

Notes

Website

Username

Password

Notes

Website

Username

Password

Notes

Website

Username

Password

Notes

Website

Username

Password

Notes

CD

Website

Username

Password

Notes

Website

Username

Password

Notes

Website

Username

Password

Notes

Website

Username

Password

Notes

Website

Username

Password

Notes

Website

Username

Password

Notes

Website

Username

Password

Notes

Website

Username

Password

Notes

Website

Username

Password

Notes

CD

Website

Username

Password

Notes

Website

Username

Password

Notes

Website

Username

Password

Notes

Website

Username

Password

Notes

Website

Username

Password

Notes

Website

Username

Password

Notes

Website

Username

Password

Notes

Website

Username

Password

Notes

Website

Username

Password

Notes

Website

Username

Password

Notes

Website

Username

Password

Notes

Website

Username

Password

Notes

Website
Username

Password

Notes

Website
Username

Password

Notes

Website
Username

Password

Notes

Website

Username

Password

Notes

Website

Username

Password

Notes

Website

Username

Password

Notes

Website

Username

Password

Notes

Website

Username

Password

Notes

Website

Username

Password

Notes

Website

Username

Password

Notes

Website

Username

Password

Notes

Website

Username

Password

Notes

GH

Website

Username

Password

Notes

Website

Username

Password

Notes

Website

Username

Password

Notes

GH

Website

Username

Password

Notes

Website

Username

Password

Notes

Website

Username

Password

Notes

Website
Username

Password

Notes

Website
Username

Password

Notes

Website
Username

Password

Notes

Website

Username

Password

Notes

Website

Username

Password

Notes

Website

Username

Password

Notes

Website

Username

Password

Notes

Website

Username

Password

Notes

Website

Username

Password

Notes

Website

Username

Password

Notes

Website

Username

Password

Notes

Website

Username

Password

Notes

Website

Username

Password

Notes

Website

Username

Password

Notes

Website

Username

Password

Notes

IJ

Website

Username

Password

Notes

Website

Username

Password

Notes

Website

Username

Password

Notes

Website

Username

Password

Notes

Website

Username

Password

Notes

Website

Username

Password

Notes

IJ

Website

Username

Password

Notes

Website

Username

Password

Notes

Website

Username

Password

Notes

Website

Username

Password

Notes

Website

Username

Password

Notes

Website

Username

Password

Notes

IJ

Website

Username

Password

Notes

Website

Username

Password

Notes

Website

Username

Password

Notes

IJ

Website

Username

Password

Notes

Website

Username

Password

Notes

Website

Username

Password

Notes

IJ

Website

Username

Password

Notes

Website

Username

Password

Notes

Website

Username

Password

Notes

Website

Username

Password

Notes

Website

Username

Password

Notes

Website

Username

Password

Notes

Website

Username

Password

Notes

Website

Username

Password

Notes

Website

Username

Password

Notes

Website

Username

Password

Notes

Website

Username

Password

Notes

Website

Username

Password

Notes

Website

Username

Password

Notes

Website

Username

Password

Notes

Website

Username

Password

Notes

Website

Username

Password

Notes

Website

Username

Password

Notes

Website

Username

Password

Notes

Website

Username

Password

Notes

Website

Username

Password

Notes

Website

Username

Password

Notes

Website

Username

Password

Notes

Website

Username

Password

Notes

Website

Username

Password

Notes

Website

Username

Password

Notes

Website

Username

Password

Notes

Website

Username

Password

Notes

Website

Username

Password

Notes

Website

Username

Password

Notes

Website

Username

Password

Notes

Website

Username

Password

Notes

Website

Username

Password

Notes

Website

Username

Password

Notes

Website

Username

Password

Notes

Website

Username

Password

Notes

Website

Username

Password

Notes

Website

Username

Password

Notes

Website

Username

Password

Notes

Website

Username

Password

Notes

Website

Username

Password

Notes

Website

Username

Password

Notes

Website

Username

Password

Notes

Website

Username

Password

Notes

Website

Username

Password

Notes

Website

Username

Password

Notes

Website

Username

Password

Notes

Website

Username

Password

Notes

Website

Username

Password

Notes

Website

Username

Password

Notes

Website

Username

Password

Notes

Website

Username

Password

Notes

Website

Username

Password

Notes

Website

Username

Password

Notes

Website

Username

Password

Notes

Website

Username

Password

Notes

Website

Username

Password

Notes

Website

Username

Password

Notes

Website

Username

Password

Notes

Website

Username

Password

Notes

Website

Username

Password

Notes

Website

Username

Password

Notes

Website

Username

Password

Notes

Website

Username

Password

Notes

Website

Username

Password

Notes

Website

Username

Password

Notes

Website

Username

Password

Notes

Website

Username

Password

Notes

Website

Username

Password

Notes

Website

Username

Password

Notes

Website

Username

Password

Notes

Website

Username

Password

Notes

Website

Username

Password

Notes

Website

Username

Password

Notes

Website

Username

Password

Notes

Website

Username

Password

Notes

Website

Username

Password

Notes

Website

Username

Password

Notes

Website

Username

Password

Notes

Website

Username

Password

Notes

Website

Username

Password

Notes

Website

Username

Password

Notes

Website

Username

Password

Notes

Website

Username

Password

Notes

Website

Username

Password

Notes

Website

Username

Password

Notes

Website

Username

Password

Notes

Website

Username

Password

Notes

Website

Username

Password

Notes

Website

Username

Password

Notes

Website

Username

Password

Notes

Website

Username

Password

Notes

Website

Username

Password

Notes

Website

Username

Password

Notes

Website

Username

Password

Notes

Website

Username

Password

Notes

Website

Username

Password

Notes

Website

Username

Password

Notes

Website

Username

Password

Notes

Website

Username

Password

Notes

Website

Username

Password

Notes

Website

Username

Password

Notes

Website

Username

Password

Notes

Website

Username

Password

Notes

Website

Username

Password

Notes

Website

Username

Password

Notes

Website

Username

Password

Notes

Website

Username

Password

Notes

Website

Username

Password

Notes

Website

Username

Password

Notes

Website

Username

Password

Notes

Website

Username

Password

Notes

Website

Username

Password

Notes

Website

Username

Password

Notes

Website

Username

Password

Notes

Website

Username

Password

Notes

Website

Username

Password

Notes

Website

Username

Password

Notes

Website

Username

Password

Notes

Website

Username

Password

Notes

Website

Username

Password

Notes

Website

Username

Password

Notes

Website

Username

Password

Notes

Website

Username

Password

Notes

Website

Username

Password

Notes

Website

Username

Password

Notes

Website

Username

Password

Notes

Website

Username

Password

Notes

Website

Username

Password

Notes

Website

Username

Password

Notes

Website

Username

Password

Notes

Website

Username

Password

Notes

Website

Username

Password

Notes

Website

Username

Password

Notes

Website

Username

Password

Notes

Website

Username

Password

Notes

Website

Username

Password

Notes

Website

Username

Password

Notes

Website

Username

Password

Notes

Website

Username

Password

Notes

Website

Username

Password

Notes

Website

Username

Password

Notes

Website

Username

Password

Notes

Website

Username

Password

Notes

Website

Username

Password

Notes

WX

Website

Username

Password

Notes

Website

Username

Password

Notes

Website

Username

Password

Notes

Website

Username

Password

Notes

Website

Username

Password

Notes

Website

Username

Password

Notes

WX

Website

Username

Password

Notes

Website

Username

Password

Notes

Website

Username

Password

Notes

Website

Username

Password

Notes

Website

Username

Password

Notes

Website

Username

Password

Notes

YZ

Website

Username

Password

Notes

Website

Username

Password

Notes

Website

Username

Password

Notes

Website

Username

Password

Notes

Website

Username

Password

Notes

Website

Username

Password

Notes

Website

Username

Password

Notes

Website

Username

Password

Notes

Website

Username

Password

Notes

Website

Username

Password

Notes

Website

Username

Password

Notes

Website

Username

Password

Notes

YZ

Website

Username

Password

Notes

Website

Username

Password

Notes

Website

Username

Password

Notes

Website

Username

Password

Notes

Website

Username

Password

Notes

Website

Username

Password

Notes

CREDIT CARD INFORMATION

Credit Card

Card #

1-800 #

Credit Card

Card #

1-800 #

Credit Card

Card #

1-800 #

Credit Card

Card #

1-800 #

www.ingramcontent.com/pod-product-compliance
Lightning Source LLC
Chambersburg PA
CBHW031245050326
40690CB00007B/955